VOICES INTEI

The High Price I Had To Pay 4

A PRODUCT OF THE GAME

SENTENCED TO SERVE 10 YEARS AS A NON-VIOLENT OFFENDER

A MEMOIR
BRANDI DAVIS

VOICES
INTERNATIONAL PUBLICATIONS

The High Price I Had To Pay: A Product Of The Game, Sentenced to 10 Years As A Non-Violent Offender, Volume IV

Copyright © 2017 by Brandi Davis

This book is a real-life story about the events that led to the imprisonment of author Brandi Davis. All names, although some are abbreviated, and events are true. This information in this book can be verified through public record. See United States v. Davis Docket #09-cr-20473, (United States Court for the Eastern District of Michigan, Southern Division.)

Printed in the United States
First Printing 2017

ISBN: 978-0-9976754-0-5
LCCN: 2016908097

Voices International Publications Inc.
196-03 Linden Blvd.
St. Albans, NY 11412
"Changing Lives One Page at a Time."

www.voicesbooks.com

Typesetting by: Jana Rade www.impactstudioonline.com
Cover Design by: Keith Saunders www.mariondesigns.com
Edited by: Dr. Maxine Thompson maxtho@aol.com

Dedication

This book is written in loving memory of my father Charles Davis and my son's father, Deron Gatling. May you both rest in peace.

Acknowledgements

Al-Hamdu Li-llah, "all praise to Allah." Without Him, this work would not be possible. He has carried me through the storm and showed me there is light at the end of the tunnel.

I want to thank my son Debron for standing strong with me through this struggle. You are the greatest! To my mother, Laura, I want to thank you for being the strongest woman I know. To have experienced so many loses and still stand tall through it all, without complaining, you are my hero!

To my Papi, I want you to know I have so much respect and admiration for you. You taught me so many life lessons and pointed out things no man has ever showed me. With your support, you've helped me to mature into the woman I am today. For that, I am extremely grateful.

To my sisters Choo-Choo and Lee-Lee, you already know, it's the three-sisters for life! Thank you both for holding me down. You've showed me what the true meaning of sisterhood is. Love you guys!!

To my nephews Jerry, Charles, and Baby D, and my niece Chloe, I thank you so much for the love and support you have all showed me. Every kind word, and the attention you gave me, helped me get through my bid.

To my girls Me-Me, Sonya, Lena, Alvina, Felicia, Jade, Trina and Zee you are the greatest friends I could ever have. I will never forget your kindness through my roughest times in life. I love you all!

To Stevie-J, thanks for being the big brother I never had. I am truly grateful for your kindness and support.

To my Davis Sister, Jamila, I wouldn't have been able to do this without your support. Thank you for recognizing my gifts and encouraging me to perform at my full potential. You've help to bring out the best in me. For that, I am grateful!

To Ma-Ma, words can't explain the love that I have for you. You took me in and treated me like I was your own. Any time you saw me slipping, you would quickly help me to get back in place. The bond we share through our life experiences can never be broken. I also gained 10 more brothers and sister. I love you all so much!

To Weedie and Boonie my brothers from another mother I have to Thank you both for pushing me to push me to tell my story and bring this to life. I will forever be thankful for you. I love you both so much!

To Aisha, thanks for being a true friend and holding me down throughout the years. You've played a major role in helping me with my book "Made Woman." I am extremely grateful for all your help. I couldn't have done it without you!

To all my brothers & sister who are still on lock, keep your head up. I know the struggle and believe me things are going to get brighter upon your release, just keep the faith! Remember these people can lock up our bodies, but they can never lock up our minds. Strive to use this time to be the best you can possibly be!

To all my friends at FPC Alderson, I want you to know that each and every day everyone of you had a significant impact on my life; I will never forget the times we shared throughout this journey.

A special thank you to my Muslim sisters! As-Salaama 'Alaykum! I love you all so very much. I will never forget you! We've prayed and fasted together, and shared many great times. I pray that we will be able to celebrate Eid in the free world together. Insha Allah. I will continue to keep you all and your families in my prayers.

To my Prison Sisters, Calisa, Joy E., Taii, Iris, Felicia aka Sky, Jessica, Diggs, Joy (Milk Dud), Felicia (Huron Valley), Miranda (Huran Valley), Paulette, and Donita, we've been through this struggle together and been there for each other through each other's highs & lows. The bond we share is so special. I'll always cherish each and every one of you ladies. Love you!

TABLE OF CONTENTS

CHAPTER ONE
Spoiled Rotten

"From the day I made my grand appearance, life for me was plush! From the blankets I was wrapped in coming home from the hospital, to the comfortable crib that I slept in, it was all top-of-the-line decor. I was my daddy's little princess, and he wanted the world to know it!"

I entered this world on April 8, 1982. From as early as I could remember, life was all about living well and having a good time. I grew up in a 4-bedroom home with an in-ground pool in Southfield, Michigan, which is a suburb of Detroit. My house was known as the "party house."On any given day, my parents would be entertaining guests, serving top-notch liquor and exquisite food. In the summer, we had large barbeques outside, listening to the sounds of old school R& B jams, as we swam in our large pool. Those were the good old days. I didn't have a worry in the world. Everything was handed to me. From the outside looking in, my family represented a picture perfect view of the "American dream." Yet, our family life was far from typical!

My father, Charles Davis, was a big time drug dealer, who was notorious in Detroit. He and his brother, Eddie Davis, had significant drug turf throughout the city. The young and the old looked up to my father, who was often very generous to the less fortunate. He also knew how to take care of himself. My daddy had swag that was out of this world! He drove every luxury car you could ever imagine, and he dressed impeccably in custom-made suits and alligator shoes. Known as an O.G. in the hood, he was well respected and feared. No one dared to cross Daddy. He was no joke!

My mother, Laura Davis, was a very pretty, well-kept woman, who could brighten up any room with her beauty and her confidence. She was a student of my dad, who taught her much of what she knew about raising her children with grace and dignity. Mom was 15 years younger than my dad. She loved and cherished the ground he walked on, and he treated her like a queen. Mommy got anything and everything she ever wanted from Daddy, sometimes even before she could ask. They were both madly in love.

I grew up with my older sister, Choo-Choo, who was five years older than me, and my younger sister, Lee-Lee, who was 4 years younger than me. As the middle child, I enjoyed many perks. I liked the fact that I could get along well with both of them. Growing up, I loved the attention my parents and my sisters showed me. I was often the "life of the party"when it came to my family affairs. I was the one they could lean on, and depend on for advice.

Life was all about my father's queen, my mom, and his three princesses, my sisters and I. My dad treated us all like royalty. From an early age, he bought us all lavish gifts (such as diamond jewelry and mink coats), took us to eat at the finest restaurants, and we traveled on cruises and trips all around the world. It was important to him that we each understood the value of our self-worth.

"Baby girl, you were born to be a queen. Don't let anybody tell you any different. If a man doesn't treat you like your daddy treats you, he doesn't deserve you. You're royalty, baby. Never forget that!" my dad would say with conviction.

Staring at his smooth caramel skin and gazing into his bright eyes, I fell in love with the man who brought me into this world. I idolized his every move. I couldn't wait to grow up and find a man just like my dad. He was my hero, and I was proud to be Daddy's little princess.

Some of the memories I enjoyed most as a child was going to visit my maternal aunts in California. My mother was the oldest out of her siblings. She had four sisters that were drop dead gorgeous! They all had smooth honey comb complexions, long fine hair and curvaceous bodies. Their beauty was commonly talked about, especially amongst men. This caused my mother and her sisters to be highly sought after. Each ended up dating big-time drug dealers, with an empire larger than the other.

My mother's sister, Aunt Kimmie, lived on a large estate, outside of Los Angeles, California. I couldn't wait for the summer to arrive, because I knew I would have tons of fun at Aunt Kimmie's place. She lived in what appeared to be a palace in the middle of the country. I enjoyed playing with the horses and the other animals on her farm, and driving around in 4-wheelers on her large parcels of land. When we got tired of playing on her estate, Aunt Kimmie would take us to all the amusement parks in California. From Disney Land, to Universal Studios and Six Flags, we made our way on every ride. When we were tired of riding, we shopped until we dropped. Anything and everything we wanted, Aunt Kimmie provided, courtesy of her drug dealer husband's large wages. When I was with Aunt Kimmie I felt like I was in heaven, so much so that I didn't want to go home!

My experiences with all my aunts were similar. They each showered us with love, attention and gifts from their lover's stash. This experience caused me not only to admire my dad, but also my mother and her sisters. In my eyes, they were the baddest chicks in the land and I wanted to grow up to be just like them!

They had no cares in the world and could shop as much as they liked. They were living the life! The common denominator for each of their success stories was the presence of a big-time hustler in their lives. Watching them, I knew just what I wanted. I couldn't wait until I grew up and got my chance to shine too! The crazy part is I knew back then my wish would come true, but I just didn't know the high price I had to pay!

CHAPTER TWO
Little Miss Pretty Girl

"Like my daddy used to say, 'His pretty little girl would become a star.' His words never left my mind. I was just waiting for the moment to show him just what his 'pretty little girl' was made of!"

From the time I was a small child, people around me complimented me for my looks. "Awe, she is such a pretty little girl," they would often say and I would smile back. I enjoyed being the center of attention. I quickly learned my looks and innocent smile could get me the things I wanted in life, so I took heed!

Although my mother dressed me in dainty outfits and frilly dresses, I was a tomboy at heart. I loved playing outside, climbing, jumping and fighting with the boys in my neighborhood. Hanging with them was fun and just felt plain natural. Athletically inclined, I enjoyed running track and playing on my Junior High School basketball team. Yet, I could switch up at the drop of a dime. With the same enthusiasm, I would throw on my cute little cheerleading outfit, grab my pom-poms and cheer for the boys. So, I kept balance.

As a child, my parents had me participate in several different activities. My mother was present at all my sports activities and she was a companion on most of my school trips. As a stay-at-home mom, whenever I needed her, she was always there. Not only could I share my life experiences with her, she supported everything I ever applied myself to do. I was always grateful for that!

Life started off great until I reached middle school years. When puberty hit, things in my world swiftly changed. The boys that I was accustomed to hanging out with, mysteriously became attracted to me. As a direct result, the girls I went to school with began to envy me. They no longer wanted to be friends with the "pretty little girl" who was used to being the highlight of the show. Instead, they wanted to fight me, because the boys they liked were more attracted to me. This caused a whirlwind of confusion in my life.

In middle school I grew tired of the "pretty little girl" image that began to haunt me. I wanted to be liked. And more importantly, I wanted to be respected! For some reason, the chicks in my school let my pretty face fool them. They thought they could say whatever they wanted and bully me. But, I wasn't having it!

"Look at Little Miss Pretty Girl. Too bad she's nothing but a punk,"one bully teased. Before the girl could finish laughing, I had knocked her down on the floor and stomped her profusely, so everyone could see. Stopping them dead in their tracks, I began to fight anyone and everyone who attempted to disrespect me. Quickly, my fight game and my no nonsense policy gained me respect. But, it also got me kicked out of the Southfield Public School System.

Labeled as being a pretty, feisty girl, with a short-temper, my parents had no choice but to enroll me in private school. I started at Shrine Academy, but that didn't last long, either. After getting kicked out of multiple schools back-to-back, prior to reaching high school, my parents decided to put me in a strict all girl school. I immediately rebelled!

Back then, you couldn't tell me anything, because I knew it all. On top of that, my long hair, smooth skin and newly matured figure helped me catch the eyes of many boys, and even men. From my past experiences, I knew I could use what I had to get what I wanted, so I tried my hand in the dating game.

Although my dad was a well-known hustler in the streets of Detroit, he didn't want my sisters or myself to have anything to do with street life. Therefore, we were forbidden to hang out in the city.

Detroit was separated by the 8 Mile strip, which was the border of the hood and the suburbs. Rebelling against my parents and what I believed to be strict, stupid rules, I decided I was going to defy their orders. Catching a ride with older friends from my neighborhood, we decided to go hang out on the East side of Detroit, in the ghetto.

From the first day I planted my feet on the ground of the inner city, I fell in love. I liked the traffic, the noise and watching hustlers in action. They intrigued me, just like my dad. These dudes weren't living off of their parent's money, like we did. Instead, they made their cash selling drugs on the block. Instantly, the excitement of having my own drug dealer as a boyfriend flooded me. As my luck would have it, my confidence and good looks landed me just what I always wanted!

Before I entered high school, I was dating an older boy. He used to let me drive around town in his Pontiac Grand Am, although I didn't even have a driver's license. Staring at myself in the rearview mirror of his car, I was delighted by the reflection I saw and what I felt it represented. I adjusted my seat and leaned back slightly, just like I watched my Auntie Kim do when she drove her drug dealer boyfriend's cars. It wasn't a Mercedes Benz or BMW like she had, but I knew I was on my way!

I did my dirt, but I dipped and dodged so my parents wouldn't detect what I was really up to. While driving one day in the hood, my heart raced when I noticed my dad. My stomach bubbled with anxiety, as he stood within a foot from me. I knew for sure the gig was up and my dad would kill me! To my surprise, he didn't even recognize me. I guess he figured his daughter would never be in his neck of the woods, but, he was wrong!

By the time I reached high school years, I was a fully-grown woman. I got good grades in school, but I was more interested in what I was going to wear to the night club on the week end. Hanging out with my sister, Choo-Choo, who was 5 years older than me, I began to meet more hustlers. Loving the attention, I used my pretty face to entice the dough boys I met, knowing I could surely get them to spend their money. Not only did I enjoy their money, I continued to spend my daddy's money, too. For my sixteenth birthday, he sent my friends, my sister and me, on an all-expense paid trip to Cancun. We had a ball! This was my first time I ever hung out with rappers and other celebrities.

To my surprise, my beauty attracted them, too! That's when it registered; there was a whole other world I was missing that was outside of Detroit. Deep down inside, I knew I was destined to make it. Like my daddy used to say, "My pretty little girl will one day become a star." His words never left my mind. I was just waiting for the moment to show him just what his "pretty little girl" was made of!

CHAPTER THREE
College Years in the "A"

"Gaining acceptance to Morris Brown College in Atlanta, Georgia, I convinced my dad to get me an apartment off campus. The first day I arrived in town, I knew I was in the place I wanted to be. Atlanta was popping!"

After I returned from Cancun, my life was never the same. The things that used to amuse me, no longer had any substance. In my mind, I knew there was a world outside of Detroit that was bigger, better and way more exciting. I just needed a plan to help me escape.

For my seventeenth birthday, my daddy bought me a brand new Chrysler 300 M. My car was maroon with shiny chrome rims. I felt proud riding in the driver's seat, knowing I was finally sporting my own car. The access it gave me led me to explore life outside of Detroit.

When it was finally time for college, I planned to head out of state. Gaining acceptance to Morris Brown College in Atlanta, Georgia, I convinced my dad to get me an apartment off campus. The first day I arrived in town, I knew I was in the place I wanted to be. Atlanta was popping! Filled with colleges, shopping centers and clubs, I had everything I needed right at my fingertips. I quickly managed to maneuver my way on the scene, frequenting all the hot night clubs.

Back then, Club 112 was everything! Lots of celebrities came through to party, along with the town's biggest hustlers. I stepped on the set dressed to impress with my expensive form-fitting dress, generously showing off my curves. Before I could settle in and order a drink, I had some of the town's finest on my heels. It took me a minute to figure out who was who, but I managed to score one of the most well-known drug dealers in the "A."

The walk-in closet of my new apartment quickly filled with brand new designer clothes, many with tags still on them. My bag and shoe collection also began to blossom. I was an official "it girl" in Atlanta, and I was proud of my accomplishment! Although my social life was busy, my grades at school weren't great. More concerned about the club scene than my education, I dropped out of Morris Brown College after my first semester.

Knowing that my parents wouldn't accept the fact I wasn't going to school, I decided to figure out a back-up plan. I researched that mortuary science was a lucrative career, so I decided to enroll at Gupton-Jones College of Funeral Services. I discovered that many people are scared to deal with dead folks, which left the door wide open for someone like me to capitalize. Learning about the composition of dead bodies and how to preserve them was intriguing, so the classes kept my attention. I figured if all else failed, I would have a good back-up plan. I'd let the dead folks take care of me!

As I excelled in school, my parents were very proud. My dad complimented me on the way he felt I was maturing. "My princess is not only pretty, she's smart too!" he would brag. Delighted with my progress, my daddy upgraded my car to a brand new white, GMC Yukon Denali XL. With my new car, I attracted even more attention in the "A."

One day I was hanging out with a few friends from college at the Shark Bar, which was a hot spot in town. Before we could order our food, the waiter came over and announced that we were being requested in the VIP section. Thrilled to be acknowledged, my friends and I curiously walked over to see who wanted to dine with us. To my surprise, it was a well-known rap artist/producer who was seasoned in the music game. He was accompanied by two other artists, one a rap super star, the other an R & B mega star, whom I greatly admired. I didn't want to give them the impression that we were groupies, so I acted as if their notoriety didn't faze me. It worked!

Immediately, the older rap producer was all over me, showering me with attention. He ordered us the most expensive entrees on the menu and kept the liquor flowing. At the end of the night, he asked for my telephone number. I slowly wrote down my digits, pausing in between our conversation, as if I was reluctant. Whatever I did, I guess it worked! The next day he was blowing up my phone to invite me to hang out at his music studio.

Walking into the large music studio in the heart of Atlanta, dressed in high-end designer gear with large Chanel glasses covering my eyes, I was ready to explore the hip-hop entertainment world. I couldn't help but to notice the numerous gold and platinum plaques that covered the walls. As I opened the door of one of the studio rooms, rap music boomed loudly and the smell of weed filled the air. The producer was behind the board instructing the rap artist I had seen the day before to repeat his second verse. I was amazed as I saw how the music I loved so much was actually made.

Discovering that I liked the music world, I often hung out at the studio during my free time. As the days went by, I became closer to the rap producer, who eventually became a good friend. Having him as an alliance, boosted my confidence even more. I knew at that point, regardless of the status a man had, or the money he made, I had the ability to catch his attention. Having this power, I decided to take my time and figure out just who would win this trophy over!

Out on the town, spending money that my father freshly wired me, I ran into two of my old friends, Chill and Black, from Southfield. I was happy to see two familiar faces, which reminded me of the good ole days back at home. Chill invited me to hang out with them at the Gentlemen's Club, a notorious strip club in Atlanta, and I agreed. When I entered the doors of this sinful paradise, I witnessed a scene I never experienced before!

Naked women danced provocatively around the crowded club, as Chill and his entourage showered dollars all over their bodies. As I approached the table where Chill and his friends were sitting, piles and piles of money were stacked on top of all the tables in their section, and bottles of Cristal flowed as if they were orange juice. I quickly noticed the familiar faces of legendary drug dealers from my hometown. They had the club on smash, so much so that all the dancers were circling only around them.

Big booty girls shook their bodies rhythmically to the beat of the popular club music that blasted through the speakers. Every time they bent over and bounced, Chill and his friends flooded them with more money. "Making it rain," so to speak, was an understatement. Each girl went home with thousands of dollars that night, courtesy of Chill and his crew, which was known as the Black Mafia Family aka BMF. From the moment I entered the club, Chill and his friends showed me mad love. They all knew who my daddy was and respected me as the O.G.'s daughter.

"Would you like a drink, baby girl?" Meech, a tall handsome, caramel-complexioned male, who was a leader of the organization, politely asked.

"Yes, I'll take a glass of Grey Goose and orange juice on ice, if you don't mind." I responded.

"Nah, we only drink bottles here. Only the best for you and your friend's baby girl," he said as he ordered me and the girls each our own bottle of Cristal. Instantly, my eyes lit up. I realized I had just been introduced to the "crème of the crop," as far as hustlers, during my era, were concerned. I'd seen many men spend lots of money in my life time. But, nothing EVER like that!

CHAPTER FOUR
BMF 4 Life

"The BMF crew had loyal soldiers who governed and controlled the drug markets in their areas. Creating a money making machine, run like a Fortune 500 company in the business world, the BMF crew made millions of dollars each month through their highly organized drug enterprise."

I t was 2001, and I had become a seasoned veteran on the social scene in Atlanta. Back then, life for me was all about partying and having a good time. I hung out with many ballers and celebrities, and we had fun. But, there was nothing that could compare to the experience I had when I started hanging out with the Black Mafia Family, aka BMF.

The BMF crew was led by two brothers who were notorious drug dealers from Detroit. They were not your typical dough boys who sold a few rocks on the block, or who distributed a couple of kilos. Both brothers had brilliant minds that could compete with the likes of Harvard Business School graduates, yet they were street dudes. Instead of killing each other for drug turf, they made strategic alliances in the street with other notorious hustlers. Collectively, they built a drug enterprise that extended through Michigan to Missouri, Georgia, Texas, and even as far as California. In each area, the BMF crew had loyal soldiers who governed and controlled the drug markets in their areas. Creating a money making machine, run like a Fortune 500 company in the business world, the BMF crew made millions of dollars each month through their highly organized drug enterprise.

After running into Chill and Black, I was taken in as family by the BMF crew. I can remember vividly the first time I went to the legendary "White House," which was the headquarters of the organization, and the home of one of the leaders Big Meech aka Za. Even before I entered the estate, I was blown away! This mansion was located on a well-manicured block, in a gated-community, located in Lithonia, a suburb outside of Atlanta. It was a huge white property that was lavishly decorated, like one of the homes you would see on "MTV Cribs." When I entered and looked around, it far exceeded any expectations I had for the home of any street hustler. The mansion was professionally filled with distinguished, modern furniture and expensive art, all matching the organization's black and white theme. Before I could sit down, I was offered champagne and catered southern food. It was clear these guys knew just how to entertain their guests. Immediately, I felt at home.

I was particularly impressed by the generosity of Meech. He reminded me a lot of my dad. Instead of keeping his wealth to himself, as he easily could have, he enjoyed sharing with others. He was one of those rare people on this earth that got pleasure simply from making others happy. Meech had a brilliant mind that could often see what others couldn't, which was his gift. His authentic genuineness and his way with words enabled him to make everyone he met feel like they were a part of his family. Being so far away from my real family, and missing them, made me cherish the love I received from my new BMF family. I became "Lil Sis" to the boys and they immediately started taking care of me. When they shopped, I shopped, too. When they went out of town, when I wasn't in school, I went, too. In a matter of months, we became inseparable. As a result, my whole life was consumed with hanging out with my brothers. During that season of my life, almost every night was a party, and I was sure to be included!

One of the perks of being down with BMF was my extended traveling privileges. The BMF's enterprise stretched across the United States. In every state where they were getting money, they also had a mansion with a driveway full of high-end, luxury cars. Often after boarding private jets, or even 747 planes, limos and luxury vehicles, such as Rolls Royce Phantoms and Maybachs, would be at the airport to pick up BMF members. Everywhere we went, there were always top of the line accommodations awaiting us. Hanging with them, I received attention and treatment like a Hollywood Star. And, I loved every minute of it!

One night we flew out to Miami to attend P-Diddy's New Year's party at the Opium Night Club. Meech rented out an entire floor at the Fountain Blue Hotel. He came by our rooms to check on us and make sure we had all the accommodations and liquor we needed. Dressed to impressed, we all met up in the lobby where there were over a dozen stretch limousines with chauffeurs standing in front of each vehicle, waiting to pick us up. Already tipsy off the champagne that was left in my room; I was in full gear, ready to turn up!

By the time we arrived at Club Opium the invite-only party was packed. Strutting in with over 40 guests behind him, Diddy gave Meech a pound and a hug. From the moment we entered, the BMF crew stood out in their thuggish attire, which included millions of dollars of gaudy diamond jewelry. Each member wore their famous platinum chains that included a huge diamond pendant, which spelled in diamonds: BMF 4 LIFE.

Catching the attention of Diddy's guests, Big Meech instantly became the life of the party. Unzipping a Louis Vuitton Messenger bag filled to the brim with 100 dollar bills, his first order for the night was 50 bottles of Cristal. Within minutes, waiters surrounded our tables, which were tucked in the VIP section, and the whole crew geared up into party mode. When I realized our presence raised the eyebrows of well-known celebrities, who kept peeping over at our section, as if they wanted to join us, I knew the BMF crew was special.

Before the end of the night, the "best of the best" were partying alongside us. Meech decided to buy bottles for everyone, so the liquor was pouring in an unlimited supply. The deejay had the tunes going and we were all lit! Then all of a sudden a fight broke out. Grabbing my purse and trying to get away from the madness, I dropped the princess-cut diamond bracelet my dad bought me for graduation. I didn't notice it was gone until I got back into the limo.

When I discovered my bracelet was gone, I was hysterical. I just knew my dad was going to kill me. Nobody understood the pain I was feeling inside, but Meech did.

"Baby girl, don't worry about that bracelet. I'll buy you a bigger, better one tomorrow. Lil Sis, I promise," Meech said as he hugged me tightly. I didn't want a new bracelet, but the fact he genuinely felt my pain and wanted to help me meant everything.

Early the next morning, P-Diddy's security came to the hotel and dropped a bag off to Meech. When he pulled out my missing diamond bracelet, which was in the bag, I was filled with joy. I understood at that point why the boys loved him and protected him, and how he became the celebrity's celebrity. Meech is an extremely compassionate and humble human being, who has an incredibly HUGE heart. During times when I needed him most, he has been there. He taught me "loyalty isn't a word, it is a lifestyle." That's why I was riding with BMF 4 Life!

CHAPTER FIVE
Bonnie & Clyde

"I made it clear I was riding with Magic all the way. It was official. I was his Bonnie and he was my Clyde. It was us against the world!"

It was the end of 2003, Thanksgiving Day to be exact. My mother came down to visit and made an incredible holiday meal. As night time approached, I received a call from Pig, one of my BMF brothers.

"What's up, Lil Sis? Do you want to come hang out tonight?" he asked.

"Sure, Big Bro. Where are we going?" I questioned.

"I need you to come get me. Then we gonna make a stop real quick and head out to Magic City," Pig replied.

"Cool. I'll be there in a minute," I said and got dressed. I had no idea the stop we would make would change the whole course of my life!

Pig and I drove to Suwannee, a suburb outside of Atlanta. He arrived at a big house that wrapped around a quiet suburban block.

"Come in. I want you to meet my boy," Pig instructed and we got out of my truck. When Pig rang the bell we were greeted by a tall brown-skinned man, who wore a low cut and was nicely built.

"Yo, what's good? Come in," the man said and led us into his large house.

"Yo, Magic, this is my Little Sis, Brandi. Brandi, this is the big homey Magic." Pig introduced us and I shook Magic's hand.

From the moment I met Magic aka Wonnie, I knew there was something special about him, which caught my attention. He was also a part of the BMF crew. He led the crew's operation in St. Louis. Magic was a perfect gentleman that carried himself like a Gee. Hanging out with him I instantly felt safe and extremely comfortable. It was like I knew him before from a past life.

We all went to Magic City together, ready to turn up. But the club was slow that night, so Magic and I got a table in the back and chilled.

"So pretty lady, do you have a man?" Magic questioned, as he filled my glass with champagne.

"No, I ain't got a man. I'm just chilling," I responded, unable to resist my urge to smile.

"Well, I see you pushing this big truck and rocking all this jewelry. You must have a good job then," he stated.

"No, Magic. My daddy takes care of me," I proudly boasted.

"Well, maybe I need to give your daddy a break and I'll take care of you," Magic stated as he grabbed my hand and I chuckled.

As the weeks went by, I enjoyed spending time with Magic. We hung out together, almost every night, just as if I was one of the boys. Around me Magic didn't have to put on airs or try to impress me. Instead, he could just be himself. He said he liked that about me. I never whined or complained when he was away or out of town. I knew his line of business and I understood what it required in order for him to be successful, so our relationship worked. I'd be lying if I said the lavish gifts he bought me and the money he gave me didn't help me stay relaxed, cause it did. Magic lived up to his word. Almost immediately he began to pay all my bills and buy me whatever I wanted, while I still pocketed my daddy's money. More importantly, I genuinely enjoyed his company. Over time he became my best friend.

At first, we kept our relationship on the low, but that didn't last! Early one morning, J-Bo and Tho, who were also BMF members, came to Magic's crib and I had spent the night. Not knowing they were there, I headed downstairs and bumped right into them. Nobody said a word, but the look on their faces told it all! After that, the cat was out the bag, so Magic and I began to freely interact around the crew. Instead of taking trips and hanging out with just the boys, we all began to hang out together. I guess you can say we were one big happy family, and I officially became Magic's girlfriend.

One day while watching television in my apartment my phone rang.

"Hello. Is this Brandi?" a woman asked in a professional tone.

"Yes, who's this?" I replied.

"I'm a realtor. I was given your information from Magic. I'd like to make an appointment to show you a property. Can we meet?" she asked.

"Okay," I responded, dumbfounded by her request.

The following day I met with the realtor and she took me to a large house in a private community In Buckhead. After she showed me the house, she asked, "Do you like it?"

"Yes. This is a real nice spot," I replied as I looked around at the well-landscaped property.

"Well, it's yours," she stated and handed me the keys.

I stood in shock, looking at the house. Then I stared at the keys in my hands. I had been given a lot of nice presents in my lifetime, but no one ever bought me a house. When I found out the property cost over $500,000, I was really taken aback. I knew at that point, my relationship with Magic had gotten serious. Is this the one my mother and aunties said I would one day find? I questioned.

Full of excitement, I rushed into the car and called Magic.
"Hello, beautiful," he answered

"Oh, my goodness Magic. I can't believe you did this," I said with joy!

"I told you I was going to take care of you. I'm your daddy now; you don't need no one else to pay your bill. Call your father and tell him you good now. Bee, I'ma show you a life that you ain't never seen before. Trust me!" Magic stated.

I listened in disbelief. *He's got to be the one*, I thought and I smiled. Shortly after, Magic and I called my dad to let him know I was moving out of the apartment he rented for me, so I could move into the house that Magic bought me. I also told him I didn't need his money anymore, because Magic was going to take care of me.

"Well, it's up to you what you want to do, but be sure about your decision. Once I'm done cutting these checks, that's it, Brandi. I mean it! You better think hard about this," my father advised.

I thought my dad would be happy to get a break, but I guess he was concerned about the life I was signing up for. Secretly, it seemed as though Magic and my dad were both in competition. But after I made my final decision to move and have Magic support me, my dad gave us his blessing.

Daddy flew in for my 23rd Birthday party that Magic threw for me. For the first time, my dad and Magic got to have their man-to-man talk alone. I had followed in my mother's footsteps to the letter. I ended up with a notorious drug dealer, who was just like my daddy.

As a gift of his affection, Magic bought me a brand new Porsche truck, and I finally got rid of the truck my father bought me. At this point, I made it clear I was riding with Magic all the way. It was finally official, I was his Bonnie and he was my Clyde. It was us against the world!

CHAPTER SIX
When It All Falls Down

"Life was about to get complicated. The man I fell in love with, and wanted to spend the rest of my life with, was a fugitive."

It was a warm spring day in 2004. I remember it like it was yesterday. Everything in my life appeared to be going well. I had all the material things I aspired to gain as a little girl, a plush home, a brand new car, more jewelry than I could wear, and a closet full of furs and designer clothes. On top of that, I had the love of my life by my side to enjoy it!

On this particular spring day, I was extremely excited. I had just gotten my hair and nails done and was fixing myself up, waiting for Magic's return. He was on his way back home from St. Louis. Knowing he was expected to arrive at any minute, I had gotten the house in order. My cell phone rang and immediately my eyes lit up, as I saw Magic's number flash on the screen.

"Hello, baby," I anxiously greeted, hoping to hear he was back in town.

"Yo, Bee, is everything good?" he asked frantically, taking me off guard.

"Yes, everything is fine. Why wouldn't it be?" I responded.

"No, Bee, for REAL! I need you to look around outside and see if you notice anything strange," Magic instructed.

Listening to his words and delivery, I instantly got nervous. Jumping to my feet, I went to the window in front of the house to see if anyone was outside.

"No, there's nobody outside," I responded, not sure what I should be looking for.

"Well, check the back of the house. Bee, make sure no one is there!" Magic emphatically stated.

Following his instructions, I checked the back of the house and I didn't notice anything out of place.

"No, Mag, there's nobody out here. What's going on? Is something wrong?" I asked nervously.

"Listen; come meet me in the shopping center behind Houston's. Bee, I need you to be careful. Make sure nobody's following you before you stop. You hear me?" Magic said in a sharp tone and hung up.

Immediately my heart began to race, because I knew Magic was in trouble. I circled around the neighborhood several times, making sure I wasn't being followed. Then, I quickly raced to the spot where he said to meet him. Filled with anxiety, I pulled into the parking lot and within minutes Magic jumped into the passenger seat of my car. From the look in his eyes, I knew the news he was about to deliver wasn't good.

"Yo, Bee, the FEDS kicked in all my cribs this morning in St. Louis. I know they are looking for me, but I got out just in time," Magic explained.

I knew at that point, life was about to get complicated. The man I fell in love with, and wanted to spend the rest of my life with, was a fugitive.

Magic stayed in town overnight. The next day he had me drop him to the clear port where a private jet was waiting for him.

"Baby, I'm going to California to handle some business. You can't go with me now. But tomorrow, I want you to fly out to LAX and I'ma have one of my man's meet you at the airport," Magic instructed, as he peeled me off a stack of money. I kissed him and watched him depart. That night I couldn't even sleep. I prayed nothing would happen to him. At that point, I realized I never took into account the trouble or the hardships that could come with the lifestyle I had chosen. I only thought about the money and having a good time. I didn't realize in a blink of an eye, it could all be taken away.

The next day, I met Magic in California. He had already copped a crib in Tarzana that he decided to make his home. For the next several months I was back and forth, from Atlanta to California. As time passed, the nervous feeling I felt subsided. Life seemed to be back to normal. Magic was still free and making lots of money, and we still partied and had a good time. The only difference was we had changed our central location.

One day while back in Atlanta, I began to feel funny. I chalked it up to all the traveling I was doing. But, when the sickness failed to cease, I decided to check it out. After going to the store and buying a pregnancy test, I went home and peed on the stick. Lo and behold, I was pregnant. I took the test twice to be sure. Then I called Magic to tell him the news.

"Damn, Bee," Magic said. "You know I'm on the run. I'm facing like 20 years if I get caught. I don't want to leave you by yourself with my seed. But the final decision is up to you. Regardless, you know I'ma hold you down."

I touched my stomach and began to think about the human life that was growing inside of me. I saw flashes in my mind of me holding my new born baby proudly in my arms and playing outside with my child, watching him or her grow up. Instantly, my mind was made up, as a feeling of joy I never experienced before filled my body. I was going to be a mommy!

After I told Magic I was pregnant, he tried his best to spend even more time with me. The morning of May 11, 2005, Magic flew in from Cali with a few of his friends to see me. We spent the day together. Later that night, the boys went out and partied. About 5:00a.m., Magic crawled into the bed next to me and fell fast asleep, while his two friends slept down stairs.

"Yo, yo! Get up! Hurry, man, get up!" one of Magic's friends said as he banged on our door and busted in.

"What's going on, man?" Magic said, as he jumped out of his sleep.

"Yo, son, the police are at the door. They've got the whole crib surrounded," Magic's friend yelled frantically.

"Oh, man!" Magic grunted as he quickly put on his clothes.

Immediately, we all went into panic mode. The whole house was surrounded by federal agents. We were trapped inside! I knew they were coming in by force; it was just a matter of minutes. Quickly, I tried my best to stash my jewelry, while Magic slipped out the bedroom.

"Put your hands up! You're under arrest!" A swat team of federal agents yelled as they barricaded through the door, with their guns out.

"Please, please, don't shoot. I'm pregnant," I shouted with my hands held high.

The officer cuffed me and ushered me outside. As I got to the front lawn, I saw Magic's friends in handcuffs, but I didn't see Magic.

"Where's Deron Gatling? We know he is in here. Where is he?"The agents demanded, but none of us would talk. They had searched the whole house and Magic was no place to be found. I said a silent prayer.

Seated out on the lawn, waiting for the officers to complete their search, we all hoped Magic had gotten away.

"Pow, pow, pow!!!" was the sound we heard, as bullets began to fly over our heads.

"Get down, get down!!!" the agents yelled and we all got down on the ground and the agents fired back.

My heart began to race. I was hoping that Magic was not killed in the cross fire.

"Who did you guys call? Did you send someone to shoot at us?" one of the agents yelled. Then, the officers began to beat and stump on Magic's friends, who were laid out on the ground.

"Please stop! Don't beat them!" I demanded, but to no avail.

Within a matter of minutes, another officer shouted. "We got him! We finally got the infamous Deron Gatling! He was hiding in the attic, but I found him."

The officers applauded in unison. While they were slapping each other five and cheering, my heart began to ache. With tears streaming down my eyes, I watched them apprehend the love of my life.

For the first time, I questioned would I ever see my child's father in the free world again. His run was finally brought to an involuntary end!

CHAPTER SEVEN
Invitation to The Game

"My entire life I had been handed everything I ever got. Thinking of having the ability to earn my own money, finally felt good. I was looking for a real solution to keep up the lifestyle Magic provided. Now I was finally offered an invitation to the game!"

On the evening of May 12, 2005, I sat in a small holding cell at the DeKalb County Jail, playing back in my mind the events that occurred. Looking down at my swollen belly that had just started to protrude, I wondered what my unborn child would think about having both parents locked behind bars.

The U.S. Marshalls extradited Magic back to St. Louis to stand for arraignment, and I was held at the county jail on state charges. While searching my home, the agents found marijuana in the house. After refusing to cooperate, and not giving them information they wanted about Magic's operation, they retaliated. The agents had the state police charge me with possession of marijuana, since the house was in my name. After calling home and informing my mother that I was arrested, she jumped on the first plane to Atlanta to bail me out. When I was finally released late that night, I was relieved to be back in the free-world. But, I couldn't stop thinking about what was going to happen to Magic.

On the morning of May 13, 2005, the day after I bailed out of jail, the Georgia state police raided my house once again.

"BOOM!!!" They kicked in the door and another swat team came in to search. Terrified, I thought this nightmare would never end! They said that a burglary was reported, but that was simply to throw us off. I found out after the fact, they were looking for the shooters that drove-by and fired shots at the U.S. Marshalls the day before.

Devastated by the second invasion, especially with my mother present to see the chaos, I knew it was time to go. My father ordered my mother to pack the house up and bring me back to Detroit, and that's just what she did.

My whole pregnancy, I stayed at home in Detroit with my parents. Daddy took care of me and he tried his best to keep a smile on my face, but I missed Magic. I wished he could go to my doctor's appointments with me and help me pick out clothes, but that desire was far from reality. Magic was housed at the Clayton County Jail in St. Louis, awaiting his sentencing.

Every chance I could get, I would fly, and sometimes drive, to St. Louis. Magic's friend, Bay-Bay, held me down the whole time. He paid my expenses, gave me money and made sure my unborn child had everything the baby would need. Even though I was well taken care of, I still longed for Magic.

On December 13, 2005 at 10:58 p.m., I gave birth to a healthy baby boy, which I named Debron Gatling. Holding him in my arms for the first time, I instantly fell in love. As soon as he got his shots, I headed to St. Louis to take him to see his dad. Although he couldn't touch him or kiss him through the glass window in the county jail visiting room, his huge smile filled with adoration made my day!

The whole time Magic was locked up, I had faith that some kind of miracle would happen and he would return home to us shortly. I wouldn't let my thoughts accept anything less. When he finally was sentenced, my world came crashing down. It was just like he predicted; he was sentenced to serve 20 years in federal prison. Around that same time, Bay-Bay got locked up, too, so the financial support I was accustomed to getting slowed down. Times were rough, but I was determined to stay strong and try my best to hold Magic down. I remember my visit to the Atlanta United States Penitentiary in July of 2006, when my son was 7 months old. It was the first time Magic got to hold Debron in his arms. He was such a proud dad. He held on to our son tightly for the whole visit.

Finally, face-to-face, without glass windows in between, Magic assured me he had things lined up so Debron and I would always be straight. It felt good to hold his hands and stare in his eyes. In my heart, I felt things would finally be okay.

It was September 9, 2006, and my day was off to a bad start. Debron cried continuously that day, so my mother and I took him to the Emergency Room. to see what was wrong. As we waited in the crowded hospital, my telephone rang. Before I could answer, I got a funny feeling down in my gut. Shaking Debron gently on my knees, attempting to quiet him down, I answered. It was Magic's sister, Trina.

"Brandi, Brandi! Did you hear what happened?" she asked as she sobbed uncontrollably.

"No, Trina. What happened?" I asked, but before she could answer, I instantly began to cry.

"It's Magic, Brandi. He's dead!" she bellowed, as she cried loudly.

"Dead! No, no, Trina. It can't be true! No, he's not dead!" I shouted and passed Debron to my mother, who was also crying.

At that moment, I lost it in the middle of the Emergency room. Doctors and nurses began running around trying to see what was wrong. I couldn't stay sober on the phone long enough to get the full details. All I knew was my child's father, who was also my best friend, was dead. To think my baby would grow up without his father devastated me even more. Every time I thought about what Magic's absence would mean to both Debron and me, I cried even more. I later found out that Magic had an asthma attack in his cell. After receiving poor treatment from the prison staff, too late, he died.

Dealing with the loss of Magic was one of the hardest things I ever had to deal with in my life. It took me several months after he was buried to finally adjust. Everything seemed to have hit all at once. Now I had to plan how I would move ahead without him, especially since he was the one making sure I was straight, even from behind bars.

While mourning at my parent's home, I got a call from my friend, J.T. The summer before, while attending one of my friend's barbeques, I met him. He knew what I was going through with Magic being locked up, so he showed his support. J.T. was a hustler from Chicago who was mad cool. He knew my heart was with Magic, and he always seemed to respect that.

J.T. called and said he was coming in from Chicago and asked if we could go out. I thought it would be a good idea to finally go outside and have a little fun, so I could break out from my depression. Enjoying the presence of his company, J.T. and I began to hang out even more, and he began to comfort me. It felt good to be able to share my feelings with someone and just release. As time went on, we both got extremely close, and eventually we became intimately involved.

He was no Magic, but he did his best to support my lavish lifestyle, which he knew I had grown accustomed to. As we spent more and more time together, he helped to ease the sting I felt dealing with Magic's death.

A few years had passed, and the New Year of 2008 had just come in. J.T. came to Detroit and he looked stressed.

"What's wrong, J.T.? You don't look like your normal self. Is everything okay?" I questioned.

"Man, Brandi, things are super-hot in Chicago right now. I'm stuck with this work and I got to try and move it," he said with frustration.

"Well, how much work is it?" I questioned, trying to think of a solution.

"I got 30 kilos of good coke I got to move right away. Brandi, I know you know a lot of people. Do you think you can help me move it?" he asked.

Quickly, I ran down in my mind all the people I could reach out to and see if they needed any work. "Yeah, I'll move 'em for you. If it's good product, it should be no problem," I replied, happy that I could potentially help J.T. out of a jam.

Within two days after J.T. dropped off the work, I had all his product sold. With over $900,000 in cash stacked up in my bedroom, I called J.T. on his cell phone.

"What's good, Brandi?" J.T. answered.

"Yo, that's done," I replied, trying to be cautious with my words over the phone.

"That's done?" J.T. questioned in disbelief.

"Yah, you heard me. It's done. Come see me," I said proudly and hung up the phone.

J.T. immediately made his way back to Detroit.

"Here you go. Here's all your money," I said, passing him two large duffle bags filled with cash.

J.T. stared at the cash in disbelief. "Yo, you are a bad chick, Brandi. I see why ole boy wifed you up. You're not only pretty; you're about your business, too! That's what's up," J.T. said and I smiled proudly. Then, he broke me off with a brick of money for myself.

I never sold drugs a day in my life, but I knew the players to call who could help me. *Maybe this will be the way I could really get back on my feet,* I thought, as I stared at the large sum of money J.T. had given me.

"Baby girl, I think me and you can work together. What you think about getting into the game?" J.T. asked.

My entire life I had been handed everything I ever got. Thinking of having the ability to earn my own money, finally felt good. I was looking for a real solution to keep up the lifestyle Magic provided. Now I was finally offered an invitation to the game!

CHAPTER EIGHT
All About the Benjamins

"With the Benjamins rolling in, nothing I wanted was off limits. J.T. bought a Ferrari cash and he got me a new Range Rover Sport. Life was all about getting money and partying....The good times were back and I enjoyed every minute of it!"

In early 2008, life as I knew it, changed substantially. J.T. and I joined forces, and within a matter of days, the money started pouring in. I never realized how powerful my contacts were, because I never needed them. Without Magic around to support me, I decided to try my hand in the game.

What I was doing was actually easy. J.T. simply asked me to hook him up with the dudes I knew who were copping major weight. After I introduced him to my people, he took over and I fell back. I never had to deal with any of the details of the drug transactions, except for the first time. But after that, all I had to do was pick up the money my homies owed on consignment.

J.T. wasn't doing it like Magic, nor did he have swag like him. But, he was plugged. J.T. had a major international drug connect that supplied him with hundreds of kilos of cocaine on consignment. With that kind of work, he needed key distributors, loyal people who could move product in a few days. Knowing he could easily be killed, with that type of money at risk, J.T. didn't just trust anybody. I knew off the rip, my people could make it happen, and I could trust them, so I put J.T. on.

From day one, J.T was hitting me with money. But, once I made the connections for him to establish his presence in Detroit, he began to break me off with larger sums, more than I had ever been given before! Watching the cash pile in; I wished I would have gotten into the game sooner. Magic always protected me from it. He would never allow me to see or touch any work. Not J.T, he wanted me to be hands on. I looked at it as he was showing me a way that I could support myself on my own, if something ever happened, so I was all in. As a result, I went from getting my bills paid, receiving lavish gifts and 10 stacks here and there, to being broke off with hundreds of thousands of dollars. In my mind, it was a come up!

The more money I helped J.T. get, the closer we seemed to become. He never wanted me out of his sight. Even when he went out of town, he took me everywhere he went. I started to question was he genuinely into me, or did he simply like the money I brought him. It was all confusing to decipher because most of our time was spent counting and collecting millions of dollars.

As J.T. and I became more serious, I introduced him to my family. Everyone seemed to like J.T. He was generous to everyone. The more money he made, the more cash he broke me off with. I finally had enough money to cop a townhouse in the suburbs of Canton, Michigan. With the Benjamins rolling in, nothing I wanted was off limits. J.T. bought a Ferrari cash and he got me a new Range Rover Sport. Life was all about getting money and partying. During our free time, J.T. and I would trick off thousands of dollars in the strip club, just like I used to do with Magic. The good times were back and I enjoyed every minute of it!

After J.T. started hanging around my family more, he hit it off well with my dad. They would talk for hours about men stuff, and they eventually discussed street life. J.T. had a drug supplier that seemed to have endless amounts of product. After discussing the wholesale prices, he received, my dad and J.T. ended up doing business.

Daddy treated J.T. like a son, and he treated my dad like his pops. For my father's 65th Birthday, J.T. threw him an over-the-top party for all my dad's friends and family. That's when he officially became like part of the family. Watching how good he treated everyone made my heart grow fonder towards him. *Maybe he was the one who would finally take Magic's place*, I thought.

J.T. was about to buy another car, and he said he wanted to cop me a Mercedes Benz S600. But, he needed a car connect that he could funnel the cash through. Remembering the dealership in Atlanta that Magic bought my Porsche truck from, I arranged for us to take a trip back to the "A."

Driving down in my Audi Q7 truck, which was also fully paid for, I took J.T. to get his car. Then, we stopped to get something to eat at the Atlanta Fish Market in Buckhead. While we were dining at the restaurant, the manager came over and approached our table.

"Excuse me, sir and ma'am, the police are outside. They want you to come out and talk to them, so they don't have to come in and make a scene. Will you please pay your bill and leave, so you don't bring negative attention to our establishment?" the manager whispered in a tone we could hear.

Immediately my heart began to race. *Here we go again*, I thought. Thinking quickly, I looked up at J.T, waiting for him to tell me what to do next. But, to my dismay he stood stiff, stuck in disbelief.

"Yo, J.T., what you got on you?" I immediately asked, off of instinct.

"Uh, uh, I got 'em, three ounces of weed." J.T. replied, dumbfounded, as he stuttered.

"Yo, give me that," I shouted and he passed me the weed.

"What else you got on you, J.T.?" I quickly questioned while sliding the weed into my bag.

"Uh, em. Nah, that's it," he said nervously.

"Yo, where's yah cell phones at?" I asked.

"Right here," he said, pulling out four different phones.

"Yo, pass them to me, too!" I instructed.

I peeped out the window and quickly slid to the restroom. I flushed the weed down the toilet and took the sim cards out of each of the phones. Then, I flushed them too. As discreetly as possible, I slid back to the table and began to talk to J.T., as if everything was fine.

"Just be cool. You don't know nothing," I said, noticing that J.T. was clearly shaken up. I felt if he saw I was going to hold him down, regardless of what happened, he would calm down.

J.T. and I finished our meal. Then, we went outside to see the officers, which turned out to be the DEA.

As we walked out of the restaurant, several federal agents surrounded my Audi and the new Bentley G.T., which we had freshly picked up from the dealership.

"How did you pay for these cars?" the officers immediately asked.

"I don't know what you are talking about." J.T. responded.

From the looks of things, the dealership we had gotten the cars from seemed to be under investigation, because all the questions they asked were pertaining to our vehicles. With no paper trail to prove our money to purchase the cars was legit, the DEA ended up confiscating both of our vehicles, and we were left to take a cab back to the hotel.

J.T. was relieved when the agents let us go free. From the way he handled his interaction with law enforcement, I knew at that moment he was not experienced in the game. J.T.'s true colors started to be exposed. He was far from a real street dude, like Magic was. From the looks of things, he appeared to be a square who simply had a good drug connect. After our encounter with the cops in the "A," I started to view J.T. differently. It made me realize how badly I missed Magic.

CHAPTER NINE
The Bust!

"Put your hands up! Brandi Davis, you are under arrest, one of the officers yelled, as he put me in handcuffs....Our run was finally up!"

As J.T.'s operation expanded in Detroit, we began to make more trips back and forth to Chicago, which was about a four-hour drive. J.T. and I would never ride dirty. He always had one of his people drive the drugs down, and another would take the money back up. His transport system was pretty tight. J.T. had bought several cars that had stash boxes built inside of them, so the drugs and the money couldn't easily be detected. The stash cars held approximately 27 kilos of cocaine each. As the orders came in, the trips that needed to be made increased.

One day my college friend, A.J., came to my house to hang out. She saw the way I was living and how J.T. had the money flowing in.

"Damn. Brandi, you always seem to find the good ones. I wish I was that lucky! Girl, things are rough right now. You know my parents split, so I am trying my best to hold my mother down. I really could use some extra cash. Do you think J.T. would allow me to take a few trips for him?" A.J. asked.

"Oh, no, girl! You can't do that! When you ride dirty, you're riding with your life," I adamantly replied.

"But, Brandi, the police will never know. I am in graduate school. I'll just tell them I am on my way back to college if they stop me," A.J. interjected.

"Absolutely not! I'm not going to let you risk your life like that. But, here is what I'll do. Let me hook you up with one of J.T.'s friends and you can get your money like that," I suggested.

"Okay, cool." A.J. agreed.

As promised I brought A.J. around and asked J.T. to hook her up with one of his friends. I thought the issue was settled, until J.T. approached me one night.

"Yo, your girl hit me up. She said she wanna be one of my drivers. What you think about that, Brandi?" J.T. asked.

"I already told A.J. no! I think it's a bad idea. She's not even street smart. She doesn't need to do anything like that," I responded, mad that A.J. went behind my back to ask J.T.

"Listen, Bee, I think A.J. would be a good look. She's a college student, so the police won't bother her. Besides that, I think it's time to switch up my drivers," J.T. said.

"J.T., I'm not cosigning none of this. I told you my opinion. Now y'all both are grown. Do what you want to do. But if it was me, I wouldn't do it," I responded adamantly.

Shortly after speaking to J.T., A.J. ended up being one of his main drivers and she started making good money. Feeling the need to protect her, I would often ride behind her in my own car. That way if the police got on her trail, I could swerve and distract them. Then, they would pull me over instead.

From the first few trips, I saw A.J. was reckless on the road. I told her to set her car on cruise control, 5 miles lower than the speed limit. But, A.J. refused to listen. Ole girl was speeding up and down the highway, with 27 kilos in the car. I immediately reported what she was doing to J.T, right in front of her. A.J. thought I was hating, but the truth is I was trying to save her life.

On the morning of September 23, 2008, A.J. hit me on the phone and said she left Chicago without me.

"Girl, why did you leave? I told you I was going to follow you?" I responded.

"Bee, I have some stuff to take care of, so I need to get back home," A.J. responded, frustrated that I was upset.

"Listen, A.J., you don't need to be in no rush, doing what you are doing. Yo, make sure you drive slow and hit me when you get back in town," I replied.

Later that night, A.J. called me, when I was with J.T. As soon as the phone rang, I got a funny feeling in my gut. The normal routine was for her to bring the car to us, but something inside made me change the plans.

"Hey, A.J., we gonna come to your crib later on and pick up the car. I'll hit you when we're outside," I said and hung up the phone before she could disagree.

"J.T., something ain't right. I don't think we should go over there tonight. Let's chill and get the car in the morning," I suggested.

"Nah, Bee, let's get this out of the way. Then we can chill all day tomorrow," J.T. said and I reluctantly agreed.

As we entered A.J.'s apartment complex, we had trouble getting in. For some reason the buzzer wasn't letting us into the community. Everything in my gut was telling me to leave. But, J.T. kept edging me on.

Once we got inside and I saw the stash car, I began to relax. A.J. came down and jumped in the car.

"Here, Brandi. Everything is good." A.J. said as she passed me the keys to the car.

We spoke for a few minutes, A.J. said, "Good bye," and went back in the house. Then, I hopped out the car and went to get into the stash car. Before I could start the ignition, several police officers surrounded the vehicle.

"Put your hands up! Brandi Davis, you are under arrest," one of the officers yelled, as he put me in handcuffs. They also arrested J.T., too. I made eye contact with him and shook my head, as we were both escorted into the police car. Our run was finally up!

Before the officers could put us in the back of the car, A.J. came out of her house escorted by officers who were already inside. With her head held down, she got into the back of an unmarked police car, without being handcuffed. At that moment it was blatantly clear she had set us up. Filled with distress, I wished J.T. would have listened to me. A.J. just wasn't built for this game!

CHAPTER TEN
The Double Cross

"As I read the government's documents, I sobbed uncontrollably. I couldn't believe what I read was true."

It was the evening of September 23, 2008. I had only been in the drug game less than nine months and I was facing major time in prison. Trapped in a dirty county jail, in a small town in Michigan, I was given a million-dollar bond. A.J. was caught speeding during a routine traffic stop and got jammed up. After the officer found the stash box and retrieved 27 kilos of cocaine out of the car, A.J. immediately turned state. Funny part is, she told the police the drugs were mine and didn't mention J.T. at all. As a result, he was given a mere $50,000 bond.

As I sat in the county jail, I began to think back on all the events that led me there. Tears dripped down my eyes, as the reality of the seriousness of my charges settled in. The officer told me I wouldn't be out of prison until my son, who was a toddler, was able to drive. I cried thinking of how my incarceration would also affect him. The more I began to feel sorry for myself, the more I missed Magic. If he was around, I would have never gotten myself into this big mess. I wasn't the only one shaken up; J.T. was clearly distraught, too. I prayed to God that he wouldn't flip on me, because he seemed way too nervous to be locked up with such a low bond.

A few days after we were arrested, we both went to our bond hearings together. J.T. needed approval to be released to his family and I was seeking a bond reduction. My mother and sister were both present in the court room. It appeared as two other people were also present for J.T.

J.T.'s attorney spoke first.

"Your Honor, I'm asking for your approval to release my client into the custody of his wife and his mother, who are here today in the court room to sign the bond for his release. I have all the documentation to prove the funds they intend to pay for the bond are legitimate," J.T.'s lawyer advocated.

"His wife?" I blurted out loud, and turned around to see who she was. My mother and sister also stood in disbelief. J.T. spent lots of time with all of us, and he shared a lot of things. But, he never told any of us that he had a wife!

If looks could kill, J.T. would have been dead. I grilled him as hard as I knew how. Rage filled my entire body, as I wondered what other dark secrets he was holding from me. For the rest of the hearing, I was off in a daze.

Later on, I found out the judge agreed to release J.T., and he reduced my bond to $250,000. J.T.'s wife bailed him out and my mother came and got me, after posting my bond. The state was waiting on the FEDS, but it didn't appear that they wanted the case. While out on bond, I spent as much time as I could with my son. I didn't know what the outcome would be, but I prayed for strength to endure whatever was next.

J.T. reached back out to me after we bonded out, but I was no longer feeling him. The surprising part was he still wanted to hustle, even with these hefty charges hanging over our heads. I told him I wanted nothing to do with the drug game and he was on his own. I guess he was a little upset, but he still came around.

When the state finally realized the FEDS weren't going to pick up the case, they gave me a chance to flip on J.T., but I refused. Even though he did me dirty, I was still not going to throw him under the bus. My lawyer finally came to the table with a plea. The lowest the state was willing to give me was a nine-year sentence. My attorney said that was great for the quantity of drugs they got and no cooperation. I spoke to J.T. and decided I would take one for the team. I pled guilty to the charges and they dismissed J.T.'s case. As a result, he was finally scot-free and I was scheduled to be sentenced.

It was difficult preparing for the reality of what was ahead. In Michigan, there was no such thing as good time, so I would have to serve my nine-year sentence day-for-day. J.T. dropped me a large sum of money to make sure I was good, and I prepared for sentencing day like a soldier.

It was March 2009, and I was still out on bond. It was early one morning and my son and I decided to spend the night at my friend's house. My phone rang, but I was too tired to answer. Then, it rang again, so I knew the call must be important.

"Hello," I answered half sleep.

"Brandi, the DEA just raided your parent's house, your sister's crib and your home boy's spot. They took your dad and they're looking for you!" a family friend said, frantically.

"Oh, man! Not again, I thought this was over," I said. But the truth was, it only just begun.

On May 11, 2009, I was sentenced in state court to 9 years in prison. It was exactly 5 years after Magic got sentenced in federal court. I had to turn myself in at sentencing. Shortly after, the FEDS indicted me and got me from Michigan state prison, where I was serving my state bid. My father was also charged on the indictment. I was so confused. I didn't understand what was happening. It all made no sense!

While being held in the federal holding facility, my federal attorney came to visit me. He brought along with him my discovery documents. Nothing could prepare me for what I was about to read.

J.T. got caught up in a drug conspiracy in Chicago that dealt with high ranking members of a large drug cartel. Facing a lengthy sentence, he turned into a government informant. Not only did he help to bring down half of Chicago's top distributors in the game, he also told on all of the people I hooked him up with, including my 67-year-old father and me.

I had to read the papers a second time, because I couldn't believe what I read. I thought J.T. loved me and my father. How could he hurt us like this? My whole family was in immense pain, especially with my father's incarceration. He was the heartbeat of our family. He was all of our pipelines of support.

As I read the government's documents, I sobbed uncontrollably. I couldn't believe what I read was true. The whole time I had been sleeping with the enemy. Two of the people I cared about and trusted had both betrayed me, and I never saw it coming. It was indeed a painful double cross!

CHAPTER ELEVEN
Prison Life

"Stripped away from all the material things that I once used to define my self-worth, I had to deal with the bare image I saw in the mirror. This made me realize I never got to meet the real Brandi, because she was always hidden."

On September 27, 2011, I was sentenced to serve 120 months (10 years) in federal prison for conspiracy to distribute 5 or more kilos of cocaine. That same day, my dad was sentenced to serve 96 months (8 years) in prison. After several months going back and forth with the government, my father and I decided to take a plea. The most damaging information we had against us was J.T.'s statement. He told everything! I do mean, EVERYTHING!! Some of the things he told, I don't even recall. With his testimony stacked against us, which included such vivid details we were boxed in. Thank God, my state judge had a heart. When he saw the FEDS had charged me with the same conduct covered in my original charges, he decided to dismiss my state case. The path was finally clear. I was left to serve my time in federal prison.

The hardest part about doing time in prison was being away from my son, Debron. I often thought about how life would be when I finally came home. Would he love me? Or, would he resent me for staying away so long? Knowing that he wanted me and needed me often left me in distress.

In November of 2011, I arrived at Alderson Federal Prison Camp, in Alderson, West Virginia. It is one of the oldest women's facilities in the country, famous for housing Martha Stewart. I was confined with approximately 1,000 women from all different back grounds, both white collar and drug offenders. When I started my time there, it was difficult to imagine the end. All I saw were the years I had in front of me. After I finished feeling sorry for myself, I decided I would extend my greatest effort to make the best out of my time.

It was very difficult to get adjusted to living out of a locker and only being able to spend $300.00 a month. Reality quickly sunk in; the lavish life I was accustom to was over! On top of that, we were only given 300 minutes a month for phone time, which limited my ability to be able to communicate with my family. I quickly learned in prison we are all the same. No one got more privileges then the other. During our stay, each prisoner was just another number.

Stripped away from all the material things that I once used to define my self-worth, I had to deal with the bare image I saw in the mirror. This made me realize I never got to meet the real Brandi, because she was always hidden. Behind the walls, for the first time in my life, I got to go within and do some real soul searching. It was time to get my priorities straight. Islam became an essential resource for me to get in tune with myself and my spirituality. As I worked on my self-improvement and committed to my religion, I realized I was strong, smart and could be successful without the help of a man. This discovery helped to increase my shattered self-esteem substantially.

While incarcerated, I participated in every program and class the prison had to offer. Enjoying the knowledge, I gained from business classes and college courses, I decided to enter the prison's cosmetology program. I felt by getting my cosmetology license, I could use it to start a career upon my release. I also got involved in Alderson's Fire Fighter program and the Residential Drug Program, which took twelve months off my prison sentence. Through participation, I learned coping skills and ways to dethrone my criminal thinking, which I never realized I had. Staying active helped my time of incarceration go by quickly.

Although I have to admit, something good came out of a tragic situation, it doesn't take away the pain that my family and I had to endure. With my father also being incarcerated, too, my mother and my sisters had to split their time and money to take care of us. Daddy was always the back bone of our family. With him gone, it forced all of us to mature. I often felt guilty about my father's incarceration.

I knew if I never introduced him to J.T., he wouldn't be caught up in all this mess. I even tried to take the time for my daddy. I told the prosecutors he didn't have anything to do with the operation. But J.T.'s story contradicted everything I said. Since he was a government informant that helped take dozens of people down, his statement held more weight. Consequently, Daddy had no choice but to accept a plea too. I was devastated about what happened, but he told me not to worry. My dad handled his incarceration like a real O.G. It's his strength that inspired my family to move ahead.

One of my happiest times behind bars was on visits. I enjoyed sitting down talking face-to-face with my family, with the ability to hold my son in my arms. For a few hours, I felt like I was in the free-world. Visits helped me to release my inner frustrations and escape from mundane prison life.

On my birthday, April 8, 2013, my mother, my sisters and my son came to visit me. I was excited to see them all. They traveled 8 hours to see me and I knew they were still tired from the long trip. Yet, they perked up when I entered the visiting room and we all had a good time the entire visit. The plan was from them to go back to the hotel and come visit me again the next day, but those plans were abruptly interrupted!

My mother got a call from one of her neighbors in Detroit. She said our family home, the I house I grew up in, burned down to the ground. Frantic, my family had to immediately leave West Virginia and deal with the emergency. Just when we finally started putting the pieces back together, we faced another tragic hit. In the fire, our family basically lost everything, including many memories we shared together. After receiving a settlement from the insurance company, my mother decided to move to Atlanta to get a fresh start.

As my family started to rebuild in the "A," once again we faced even more disturbing news. My father was diagnosed with dementia, and the doctors said he wasn't expected to live that long. I cried profusely hearing the tragic news. My dad had always been such a strong, healthy man, so I couldn't believe what I was hearing. Behind the walls, I felt helpless. All I wanted to do was reach out and hug my daddy, and lay in his lap, like I use to do when I was a little girl. But, I couldn't. The reality was I still had a lengthy sentence to deal with, which prevented me from helping my family when they needed me the most. The guilt that raised from this reality may take a life time to pass. It's a situation I can never change or really fix.

My father's attorneys got involved and filed for a compassionate release for my dad, so he could spend his last days of his life with his family. By the grace of God, it was granted in February of 2015, and Daddy was released from federal prison. I was so excited to hear he would spend his last days home with my family.

A few days before his release, we got Skype at the prison. I already had my first appointment scheduled, so I was able to see my father for the first time in over 4 years, just 2 days after he came home. The feeling I felt was undesirable. It was a joy I hadn't experienced in many years. Tears automatically streamed down my face as my daddy began to talk to me. Although I was happy to see him, I couldn't help but to notice that he'd aged substantially since the last time I had seen him.

"Brandi, baby is the that you?" my daddy said joyfully.

"Yes, Daddy it's me," I replied.

It was good to be able to communicate with him, but he was clearly not the same. His memory would go in and out. And, as the months went by, he started to lose his mobility. Watching him deteriorate killed me inside. I would have done anything to be home and be by his side. He needed me, but I couldn't be there. That hurt the most!

On the morning of August 13, 2015, when I started my day, inside I knew something was not right. I felt broken and sad, but I didn't know exactly why. I had a Skype visit set with my family for later that evening. I couldn't wait to get on the call, so it could help pick up my spirit.

When I saw my daddy on Skype that day, it instantly frightened me. Within 4 days he had taken a turn for the worst. Daddy laid helpless in the bed, incoherent.

"Daddy, it's me Brandi. It's your baby girl," I said desperately, trying to get his attention. But, he didn't respond.

Watching Daddy struggle to breathe, I knew he didn't have too much longer on this earth, so I began to cry out to him.

"Daddy, I love you so much. I just want you to know that you mean everything to me! Daddy, I couldn't have made it in this world without you. I appreciate everything you ever did for me and I want you to know no matter what happens in life, I will never forget you. I'm so sorry, Daddy, for everything you are going through. I love you, Daddy, with all of my heart. I swear I do!

Wherever I go, Daddy, and wherever you are, I want you to know that you'll forever be a permanent part of my heart. I promise," I said as I choked over my tears.

As I stared at his body, tears streamed down my father's face. My whole family was standing around his bed and Daddy took his last breath. It's like he was waiting for me to call before he left. I wailed loudly when they said he was dead. Reality hit like a ton of bricks. I would never see my father alive again!

CHAPTER TWELVE
The Return

"I'm not returning to the free-world with a whole bunch of money, nor do I desire a quick fix, come up. Today what I have is faith that if I do the right thing and follow a straight path, doors will open for me. Holding on to my faith, I know brighter days are ahead!"

It's May 2, 2016 and I'm preparing for my release from prison tomorrow. Right now, I am feeling so many mixed emotions, as I never expected this day, which seemed so far away, to arrive. I thought that prison would be the death of me. But, in this dark place I finally gained my wings to fly. Tomorrow, I'll take my first flight.

It's been over 7 years since I was last in the free-world. Many things have changed, so I'm not quite sure what to expect. All I know is I can't wait to hold my son, Debron, in my arms. I probably won't let him go for a while. My baby was three years old when I left; now he is ten and full of energy!

It's my goal to go home and make up for lost time. There are so many things I want to do, and so many places I wish to explore. One thing this experience has taught me is how to cherish and value even the small liberties of life. Therefore, I plan to enjoy every moment and respect my freedom, because I know what it feels like for it to be taken away.

I wrote this book because I want to warn those who dare to try their hand in the drug game, and those who think it's cool to date a drug dealer, it's all a deadly trap! Yeah, it may look good and it might feel good for a moment. But, in the end this lifestyle ONLY leads to grief! As you now know, I wasted many years of my life chasing all the wrong things, only to realize eventually it would all be taken away. On top of that, it cost me close to a decade of my life. No one really schooled me to the truth of what inevitably happens. I saw a few of the lucky ones have a long run, but even they have fallen from grace. Watching it all play out, while living the consequences, I can tell you first hand, it's not worth it! I'd do anything to rewind the hands of time, pay my dues, and live life the right way. I can't take back the past, but you can control your future. Please don't make my same mistakes!

As a mother who loves her only child dearly, I realize in many ways I failed my son by entering a lifestyle that would cause him so much pain. He wasn't looking for all the material things I wanted to buy him. All he wanted was the presence of his mother, and that was taken away. Now, due to my poor choices, I missed out on my son's first day of school, his first ball games, birthdays and too many holidays to count. The only time I have gotten to spend with him is in a crowded prison visiting room. I can't explain precisely the pain I felt, when at the end of the visits my son would ask, "Mommy, why can't I go with you?"

How do you explain to a child so young that they can't come home with their mother because she made a bad mistake? Kids just don't understand that!

By far, this hasn't been easy! But, despite the challenges my son has faced, he stood strong through it all. Losing his dad and his mom, then his grandfather, all back-to-back, has taken a toll on him. Yet, he's managed to excel and push through it all. That's why my son is my hero!

I can't wait to return to the free-world and be the good mother, I know I can be. Debron is a beast on the court! I'll be front and center, up in the stands, cheering my baby on at his games. In a few days, for the very first time, I'll finally get to see him play basketball. I can't wait!

Experiences like this teach you what counts and what doesn't. I've been blessed to have an encouraging mother and two wonderful sisters who held me down my entire bid. I can't wait to return the love they've showed me in the free-world. I also want to embrace all my friends that held me down throughout my whole bid. When we finally reunite, it's going to be awesome!

The hardest thing I know I'm going to have to deal with is the absence of my father. In prison, it is very hard to grieve, so I know I'll have to deal with the reality that my dad isn't here any longer, and he's not coming back. I know that will be difficult to cope with. Too much pain to dwell on.

One thing I am most proud of is developing a relationship with God. Today, I know regardless of what I encounter in life, I can always count on Him. It's His grace and protection that carried me through this bid.

I'm not returning to the free-world with a whole bunch of money, nor do I desire a quick-fix, come up. Today, what I have is faith that if I do the right thing and follow a straight path, doors will open for me. Holding on to my faith, I know brighter days are ahead!

I often think back on how I lost my son's father, Magic. Had he and I both chosen another path, we could have enjoyed the rest of our lives together. Did we really need all the cars, houses, jewelry and clothes? Would life have been so terrible if we didn't have a whole lot of money? One thing for sure, we both would have gotten to keep our freedom, which could have saved Magic's life.

I'm writing to warn all those that think everything that glitters is gold. When it comes to fast money, what you think you are gaining can easily cost you a high price that you don't want to have to pay! Therefore, I urge you to use my story as a warning; we all get one before facing self-destruction. I wish I would have taken heed to the warnings I got!

Be smart and measure the consequences of what you do, before you act. Regardless of how smart you think you are, fast money will always come with a hefty price I want to leave you with some jewels that I learned through my own turbulent experiences: Pursue your education, so you can support your family if your relationship ends through death, incarceration or divorce. Don't pursue men who are involved in criminal activities, because their run will surely come to an end! Never put money over your freedom, even if you think it will be a means to help your children. Instead make your presence, your time, your spiritual insight, and most importantly, your gift of love a priority over everything else. Always desire to be better and work daily on becoming the best you that you can possibly be! Self-improvement comes by reading and studying the lives of other successful people. Therefore, read your Holy book and self-help books that will strengthen and inspire you.

Last, never give up on your dreams! Regardless of how hard or far you feel you have fallen, you can always climb back to the top!

AFTERWORD
"It's Time For A Call To Action!"

#womenoverincarcerated

S pending close to a decade behind bars has been one of the most difficult experiences in my life. I am first to admit that I made many mistakes, but now that you've read my story hopefully you see clearly how my life went astray. I became a product of my environment; I did what I saw others doing around me. I had no clue at the time, my actions would cost me a ten year prison sentence in federal prison.

Behind bars, first-hand I noticed many others around me made the same mistakes. We were taught it was "cool or "cute" to date a drug dealer and live off his fast money. But no one told us our decision would cost us football numbers in prison, or even life! That is why I felt it was necessary to share my story. I wrote this book to warn others not to make my same mistakes, and to shed light on the lengthy sentences women face in the U.S. judicial system.

When people usually think of prisoners they think about just men. That is no longer the case. Women are filling prisons in this country in record amounts! Between 1980 and 2010, the number of women in prison increased 646%, rising from 15, 118 to 112,797. Today there are over 205,000 women in prisons and jails within the United States. Approximately 10% of this population is federal prisoners, many of whom are serving decade plus sentences for non-violent crimes, as first time offenders.

I am stating the facts, because it's important that light is brought to this population, which is often left without a voice. Although I am now free, I have left behind several of my prison sisters, who still have long sentences to serve. Just like myself, they were stripped away from their families and children. Consequently, their families are also serving time. In addition, this epidemic is sparking another nasty cycle of inter-generational incarceration.

Many may say this not your problem, but the truth is it is! Tax payers are spending billions of dollars to house and care for the incarcerated. Behind the walls, there are limited platforms for real rehabilitation. Therefore, prisoners are simply "warehoused," so they come back out to the free-world in a worse state than they come in. I watched this vicious cycle first hand. In a dark place, which often is lacking love, women are caged in, just sitting until their release dates. Many aren't scheduled for release for many years to come, so they feel hopeless and give up.

Even more disheartening, many of these women I am speaking of are women of color. In record amounts, black women are being severely punished by what appears to be a heartless system. I am not saying we shouldn't have to pay for our mistakes, yet is a decade plus sentence for young mothers really necessary to get the lesson? I don't think so! Given the opportunity, I believe I could have paid my debt back to society in a more productive manner, and I would have still gotten the message loud and clear.

Although I've done my time, and paid a hefty price for my mistake, I have still chosen to give back. Today I am an advocate for women who walked the same path I did. I am here to tell them there is light at the end of the tunnel. It's never too late to turn your life around. I made it, so can you my sister!

Today I plead with every American to take a closer look at our nation's judicial system, which is supposed to represent justice for all. There are thousands of women behind bars that face many injustices and are held captive, with no recourse! These women could be your neighbors, friends, co-workers or even your relatives. The FEDS don't discriminate. Next, it could be you! Therefore, it's time for a call to action! It's time to demand justice and equality for all in the U.S. judicial system, and it's time to release the many women serving decade plus sentences for non-violent crimes! Your voice can make a difference! Please speak out and help us in our plight for change.

For more information about the epidemic of
women in prison and over-incarceration,
visit www.womenoverincarcerated.org and on social media lift
us up, #womenoverincarcerated.
Together we can indeed make a difference!

About the Author

B randi Davis, born and raised in Southfield, Michigan, is an author, motivational speaker and a prison reform activist. Davis, the daughter of legendary street hustler and the girlfriend of a notorious drug dealer, was no novice to street life. After her child's father suddenly died in federal prison, she faced the challenge of maintaining the lavish lifestyle he provided. With her back up  against the wall, Davis accepted an invitation to enter the drug game and became extremely successful. Life was grand until Davis was caught red-handed with 27 kilos of freshly packaged cocaine, landing her a ten year sentence in federal prison.

After serving close to a decade behind bars, Davis has decided to share her life experiences to warn others about the danger of poor choices. With her powerful voice and bona fide street credibility, she has captivated the attention of youth and adults across the nation. Exposing the naked truth and deadly consequences of street life, her heartfelt story has become an anchor used to save the lives of many of today's troubled youth.

Voices International Publications Presents

$\mathcal{V}oices$ of
CONSEQUENCES
ENRICHMENT SERIES
CREATED BY: JAMILA T. DAVIS

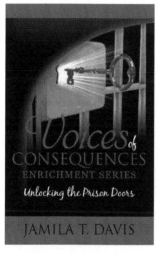

Unlocking the Prison Doors: 12 Points to Inner Healing and Restoration

ISBN: 978-09855807-4-2 Textbook
ISBN: 978-09855807-5-9 Workbook/Journal
ISBN: 978-09855807-6-6 Curriculum Guide
is a nondenominational, faith-based instructional manual created to help incarcerated women gain inner healing and restoration. In a comforting voice that readers can recognize and understand, this book provides the tools women need to get past the stage of denial and honestly assess their past behavioral patterns, their criminal conduct and its impact on their lives and others. It provides a platform for women to begin a journey of self-discovery, allowing them to assess the root of their problems and dilemmas and learn how to overcome them.

This book reveals real-life examples and concrete strategies that inspire women to release anger, fear, shame and guilt and embrace a new world of opportunities.

After reading readers will be empowered to release the inner shackles and chains that have been holding them bound and begin to soar in life!

VOICES
INTERNATIONAL PUBLICATIONS
"Changing Lives One Page At A Time."
www.vocseries.com

Voices International Publications Presents

$\mathcal{V}oices$ of
CONSEQUENCES
ENRICHMENT SERIES
CREATED BY: JAMILA T. DAVIS

Permission to Dream:
12 Points to Discovering
Your Life's Purpose and
Recapturing Your Dreams

ISBN: 978-09855807-4-2 Textbook
ISBN: 978-09855807-5-9 Workbook/Journal
ISBN: 978-09855807-6-6 Curriculum Guide
is a nondenominational, faith-based, instruction
manual created to inspire incarcerated women to
discover their purpose in life and recapture their
dreams. In a way readers can identify with and
understand, this book provides strategies they
can use to overcome the stigma and barriers of
being an ex-felon.

This book reveals universal laws and proven
self-help techniques that successful people apply in their everyday lives. It helps
readers identify and destroy bad habits and criminal thinking patterns, enabling
them to erase the defilement of their past.

Step-by-step this book empowers readers to recognize their talents and special
skill sets, propelling them to tap into the power of "self" and discover their true
potential, and recapture their dreams.

After reading , readers will be equipped with courage and tenacity to take hold of
their dreams and become their very best!

INTERNATIONAL PUBLICATIONS
"Changing Lives One Page At A Time."
www.vocseries.com

Voices International Publications Presents

Voices of
CONSEQUENCES
ENRICHMENT SERIES
CREATED BY: JAMILA T. DAVIS

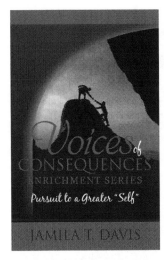

Pursuit to A Greater "Self:" 12 Points to Developing Good Character and HealthyRelationships

ISBN: 978-09855807-7-3 Textbook
ISBN: 978-09855807-8-0 Workbook/Journal
ISBN: 978-09855807-9-7 Curriculum Guide
is a non-denominational, faith-based, instruction manual created to help incarcerated women develop good character traits and cultivate healthy relationships. This book is filled with real-life examples that illustrate how good character traits have helped many people live a more prosperous life, and how deficient character has caused others to fail. These striking examples, along with self-help strategies revealed in this book, are sure to inspire women to dethrone bad character traits and develop inner love, joy, peace, patience, kindness, generosity, faithfulness, gentleness and self-control. This book also instructs women how to utilize these positive character traits to cultivate healthy relationships.

After reading readers will be inspired to let their light shine for the world to see that true reformation is attainable, even after imprisonment!

INTERNATIONAL PUBLICATIONS
"Changing Lives One Page At A Time."
www.vocseries.com

Voices International Publications Presents

Voices of
CONSEQUENCES
ENRICHMENT SERIES
CREATED BY: JAMILA T. DAVIS

**Volume #1-
Unlocking the
Prison Doors:**
12 Points to Inner
Healing and
Restoration
ISBN: 978-09855807-0-4

**Volume #2-
Permission
to Dream:**
12 Points to Recapturi
Your Dreams and
Discovering Your
Life's Purpose
ISBN: 978-09855807-4-2

**Volume #3-
Pursuit To A Greater "Self:"**
12 Points to Developing Good
Character Traits and Healthy
Relationships
ISBN: 978-09855807-7-3

Purchase your copies today!
Visit us on the web @ www.vocseries.com, or write us at
196-03 Linden Blvd. St. Albans, NY 11412

INTERNATIONAL PUBLICATIONS
"Changing Lives One Page At A Time."

NOW AVAILABLE FROM

VOICES

INTERNATIONAL PUBLICATIONS

"Every negative choice we make in life comes with a consequence. Sometimes the costs we are forced to pay are severe!"
— Jamila T. Davis

She's All Caught Up is a real-life cautionary tale that exemplifies the powerful negative influences that affect today's youth and the consequences that arise from poor choices.

Young Jamila grew up in a loving middle class home, raised by two hardworking parents, the Davises, in the suburbs of Jamaica Queens, New York. Determined to afford their children the luxuries that they themselves never had, the Davises provided their children with a good life, hoping to guarantee their children's success.

At first it seemed as though their formula worked. Young Jamila maintained straight As and became her parents ideal "star child," as she graced the stage of Lincoln Center's Avery Fischer Hall in dance recitals and toured the country in a leading role in an off-Broadway play. All was copacetic in the Davis household until high school years when Jamila met her first love Craig- a 16 year old drug dealer from the Southside housing projects of Jamaica Queens.

As this high school teen rebels, breaking loose from her parents' tight reins, the Davises wage an "all-out" battle to save their only daughter whom they love so desperately. But Jamila is in too deep! Poisoned by the thorn of materialism, she lusts after independence, power and notoriety, and she chooses life in the fast lane to claim them.

When this good girl goes bad, it seems there is no turning back!
Follow author, Jamila T. Davis (creator of the Voices of Consequences Enrichment Series) in her trailblazing memoir, *She's All Caught Up!*

ISBN: 978-09855807-3-5
www.voicesbooks.com

NOW AVAILABLE FROM
VOICES 💬
INTERNATIONAL PUBLICATIONS

"Is it fair that corporate giants get to blame 'small fries' like myself, whom they recruited but they walk away scott-free?"
— Jamila T. Davis

Years before the 2008 Financial Crisis, a major epidemic of mortgage fraud surged throughout the country. The FBI geared up to combat the problem, imprisoning thousands who were alleged to have victimized Wall Street giants, such as Lehman Brothers Bank. Hidden safely behind the auspices of being a "victim," savvy Ivy League bank executives created additional fraudulent schemes to further their profit. Utilizing their "victimizers" as scapegoats, the bankers' clever plan went undetected. Consequently, the real architects of the massive fraudulent lending schemes escaped unpunished. And the "small fries," who the bankers blamed to be the bandits, were left to do big time!

The High Price I Had To Pay is a captivating real-life story that reveals another aspect of the inside fraud perpetrated by Lehman executives that has yet to be told!

This illuminating synopsis by author Jamila T. Davis, who is currently serving a 12 1/2 year sentence in federal prison for bank fraud, is shared from a unique stand point. Davis was labeled by Lehman attorneys as the 25 year old mastermind who devised an elaborate mortgage scheme that defrauded their bank of 22 million dollars. Her shocking story captures the inside tricks of Wall Street elite and takes you up-close and personal into a world driven by greed and power.

Davis' story will leave you amazed and make you think. Have savvy Wall Street executives, such as Richard Fuld, been able to out smart the world? And while these executives escape unpunished, is it fair that "small fries," like Davis, are left to do big time?

ISBN: 978-09855807-9-7
www.voicesbooks.com

NOW AVAILABLE FROM
UOICES
INTERNATIONAL PUBLICATIONS

"To-date, I have served 16 years of the 30 year sentence that was handed down to me. I feel like I was left here to die, sort of like being buried alive!"
— Jamila T. Davis

In 1982, during a period when illegal drug use was on the decline, President Ronald Reagan officially announced the War on Drugs. In support of his effort, Congress passed bills to tremendously increase the sentences imposed on drug dealers, including lengthy mandatory minimum sentences. With drug sentences accounting for the majority of the increase, in less than 30 years, the U.S. prison population exploded from 300,000 to more than 2 million! The statistics are well known, but the true faces of those imprisoned and the effects of their incarceration is less publicized.

The High Price I Had To Pay 2, is a captivating real-life story about the life of Michele Miles, a 21 year old, African American woman, who grew up in Marcy Housing Project in Brooklyn, New York. Miles lured in by her boyfriend, Stanley Burrell, tried her hand in the drug game, as a way to escape poverty. Through what she believed to be a promising opportunity, Miles became partners in the notorious "Burrell Organization," which became a thriving enterprise. Overnight, Miles went from "rags-to-riches." In her mind, she was living the life of her dreams.

All was well until the FEDS got wind of the operation. With the help of informants, the Burrell empire swiftly crumbled and the key players were arrested, including Miles. In the end, her role in the drug conspiracy led Miles to receive a thirty year sentence in federal prison.

Miles' story gives readers an inside view of the life of women serving hefty sentences for drug crimes, and the effects of their incarceration. This story will leave you shocked about the rules of prosecution for drug offenders in the U.S. judicial system and make you think. Should a first time, non-violent offender, receive a thirty year sentence?

ISBN: 978-09911041-0-9
www.voicesbooks.com

NOW AVAILABLE FROM

VOICES
INTERNATIONAL PUBLICATIONS

"I am a 73 Year Old woman currently serving an 11 year sentence in federal prison. One bad decision landed me a decade plus sentence as a first time, non-violent offender."
— Gwendolyn Hemphill

Since 1970, the U.S. prison population has increased seven fold, growing to over 2 million prisoners. Consequently, even though it only consists of 5% of the world's population, America leads the world with the largest prison population. Crime rates are not increasing, yet the U.S. prison population continues to steadily grow. As a result, mass incarceration is a major epidemic that destroys families and costs tax payers billions of dollars each year. The statistics are well known, but the true faces of those imprisoned and the injustices they encounter in the U.S. judicial system is less publicized.

The High Price I Had To Pay, Volume 3, is a captivating true story about the life of Gwendolyn Hemphill, a 73 year old woman currently serving a 11 year sentence for her role in a scheme to defraud the Washington Teachers Union (WTU).

Rising from humble beginnings in the rural town of Johnstown, Pennsylvania, Hemphill worked relentlessly to overcome barriers of poverty and racism. Known for her savvy wit and creative political strategies, she successfully advocated for unions and political groups, including the legendary SNCC, during the era of the civil rights movement. Climbing to the top of the political ladder, as a rising star, Hemphill made her way up to the White House under the Carter Administration. For decades, she vigorously served as a liaison who provided substantial contributions to her community; making waves in the world of Washington D.C. politics. Despite her accomplishments and her stellar career, one bad decision landed Hemphill a decade plus sentence in federal prison, as a first time, non-violent offender.

Hemphill's story gives readers and inside view of the many female, white collar offenders, who are serving lengthy sentences behind bars. This story will leave you questioning is there mercy and equality for all citizens in the U.S. judicial system? And, it will make you think: Should a senior citizen with a stellar past serve a decade plus sentence as a first time, non-violent offender?

ISBN: 978-0-9911041-2-3
www.voicesbooks.com

INTERNATIONAL PUBLICATIONS

ORDER FORM

Mail to: 196-03 Linden Blvd.
St. Albans, NY 11412
or visit us on the web @
www.vocseries.com

QTY	Title	Price
	Unlocking the Prison Doors	14.95
	Unlocking the Prison Doors Workbook/Journal	14.95
	Permission to Dream	14.95
	Permission to Dream Workbook/Journal	14.95
	Pursuit to A Greater "Self"	14.95
	Pursuit to A Greater "Self" Workbook/Journal	14.95
	The High Price I Had To Pay	7.99
	The High Price I Had To Pay 2	7.99
	The High Price I Had To Pay 3	9.99
	She's All Caught Up	14.95
	Total For Books	
	20% Inmate Discount -	
	Shipping/Handling +	
	Total Cost	

* Shipping/Handling 1-3 books 4.95
           4-9 books 8.95
* Incarcerated individuals receive a 20% discount on each book purchase.
* Forms of Accepted Payments: Certified Checks, Institutional Checks and Money Orders.
* Bulk rates are available upon requests for orders of 10 books or more.
* Curriculum Guides are available for group sessions.
* All mail-in orders take 5-7 business days to be delivered. For prison orders, please allow
  up to (3) three weeks for delivery.

SHIP TO:
Name: _____
Address: _____

_____

_____

City: _____

State: _____ Zip: _____